$9-11-90$

To my Heart friend ~

   Your birthday is the perfect time
To celebrate You & LOVE & friendship...
   We are so fortunate to be On This
journey thru life Together - So Many
Moments - So Many Memories - The curves
& the straight PATHS - the Highs - the Lows -
the easy, the difficult - the Sublime - the
Supreme - all the experiences of life
shared with the gift of a Unique friend.
become richer - clearer & more defined -
the gift of friendship - Yours - Mine -
has been enhanced because We give
thanks to Our Creator & what better
day - Than Your birthday - all Creation
shouts with Joy Happy Birthday ~

THE
HEART
OF
LOVE

The HearT is not judged
by How Much You Love -
But by How Much You
are Loved by Others

the Wizard of OZ

Love & Peace Marva -

First published in Great Britain in 1987
by Macdonald & Co (Publishers) Ltd

Compilation copyright © Macdonald & Co
(Publishers) Ltd, 1987

This book was created by
Eldorado Books Limited, London,
and was designed by Linda Cole.
The illustrations are the work of
Russell Barnett, Bev Brennan, Grahame Corbett and Sally Kindberg.

Library of Congress Cataloging-in-Publication Data
The Heart of love.
    1. Love – Literary collections.   I. Young, Priscilla
PN.6071.L7H4 1987 808.8'0354 86-14287
ISBN 0-06-015675-9

Printed in Great Britain

To be alone with you
 At the close of the day
With only you in view
 While evening slips away.
It only goes to show
 That while life's pleasures be few,
The only one I know
 Is when I'm alone with you.

Bob Dylan

My Love draws near with airy tread,
  And glances shy and sweet;
Sing, little bird, above her head,
  Bloom, flowers, beneath her feet.

A tiny moon as small and white
    as a single jasmine flower
Leans all alone above my window,
    on night's wintry bower,
Liquid as lime-tree blossom, soft
    as brilliant water or rain
She shines, the first white love of
    my youth, passionless and in vain.

D. H. Lawrence

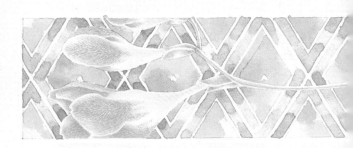

St Valentine's Day commemorates the
martyrdom of a Roman priest who was put to
death in 270 AD because of his Christian beliefs.
Its link with love goes back to the Roman festival
of Lupercalia, which was intended to promote
fertility and banish evil. With the spread of
Christianity, pagan customs were replaced by the
observation of saints' days and this was how
St Valentine, killed on the eve of Lupercalia,
entered the calendar. By this time Lupercalia had
become known as the Spring Festival, and so
St Valentine's Day also serves to celebrate the
time of year when, as Tennyson wrote, 'a young
man's fancy lightly turns to thoughts of love'.

From about the 15th century the custom grew on St Valentine's Day of sending a sweetheart or special friend a present, accompanied by words of endearment. From this there developed the giving of valentine cards, which became a popular expression of affection in Victorian times and lingers on to this day.

You are the smile of a summer's day,
The perfume of a sweet bouquet,
Your eyes a beacon gleaming bright,
All lit by Love's eternal light.

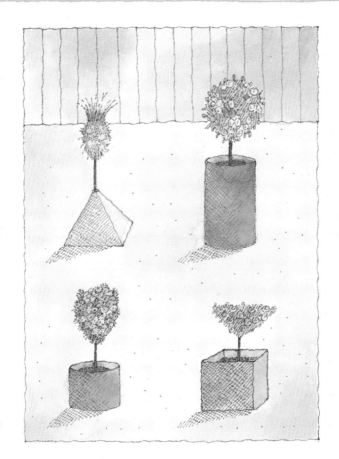

Do you exist
my pretty bird
flying
above the snows?

Are you actually
flying
or do I imagine
it so?

Detail of wing
and breast
unquestionably
there –

Or do I merely
think you
perfect
in mid-air?

William Carlos Williams

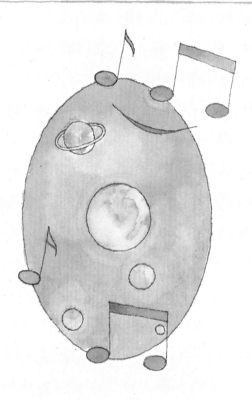

Sing, for Faith and Hope are high,
   None so true as you and I.
Sing the Lovers' Litany:
   'Love like ours can never die!'

Rudyard Kipling

Variegated tulip

beautiful eyes

Daisy

innocence

American cowslip   *divine beauty*

Rose   *true love*

In the course of many centuries, flowers came to be associated with a range of human virtues, vices and emotions. In Victorian times the Language of Flowers was formalized and was widely used in illustrations for all manner of greeting cards. So it is that flowers are rich in romantic meaning.

Love thou thy dream
   All base love scorning,
Love thou the wind
   And here take warning
That dreams alone can truly be,
   For 'tis in dream I come to thee.

Ezra Pound

· The Heart ❤ of Love ·

Love is patient, love is kind.
    It does not envy,
it does not boast, it is not proud,
it is not rude, it is not self-seeking,
    it is not easily angered,
it keeps no record of wrongs.
Love does not delight in evil
    but rejoices with the truth.
It always protects, always trusts,
    always hopes, always perseveres.
Love never fails.

I Corinthians Chapter 13
New International Bible

25

Love you forever and forever.
Love you with all my heart.
Love you whenever we're together.
Love you when we're apart.

John Lennon and Paul McCartney

I will make you brooches and toys for your delight
    Of bird-song at morning and star-shine at night.
I will make a palace, fit for you and me,
    Of green days in forests, and blue days at sea.

I will make my kitchen, and you shall keep your room,
   Where white flows the river and bright blows the broom,
And you shall wash your linen and keep your body white
   In rainfall at morning and dewfall at night.

Robert Louis Stevenson

If you agree to be my love
   I'll pledge myself to you.
We'll live together harmoniously
   Our whole life through.

Friends will come and share our joy
   On our appointed day,
When we commence our life anew
   On life's romantic way.

Sweet honey comes from bees that sting,
  As you are well aware;
To one adept in reasoning,
  Whatever pains disease may bring
Are but the tangy seasoning
  To Love's delicious fare.

Richard Wilbur

I send you red, red roses
To tell you of the morn,
When first among the roses
Our happy love was born.
I send you white, white roses
To tell you of the night,
The night in all its beauty
With all its dreams and light.

And when you see the roses,
This will the roses say:
There is no day without you,
No night when you're away,
No day I do not love you,
No night I do not pray
That God will bless and guard you,
For ever and a day!

Fred E. Weatherly

I can't think of any other way
    To tell you how I feel,
Except to say what I hope you know –
    I love you so.

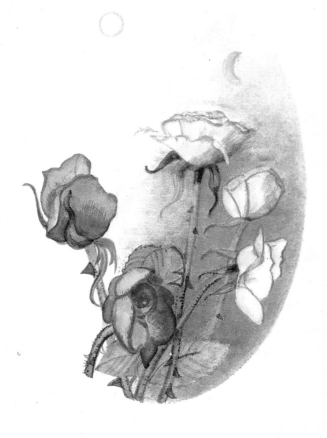

No matter what trials may beset you
On life's unpredictable way,
You can always count on my love for you
Through each and every day.

My heart is like a singing bird
   Whose nest is in a watered shoot;
My heart is like an apple tree
   Whose boughs are bent with thickset fruit;
My heart is like a rainbow shell
   That paddles in a halcyon sea;
My heart is gladder than all these
   Because my love is come to me.

Christina Rossetti

The night has a thousand eyes,
  And the day but one;
Yet the light of the bright world dies
  With the dying sun.

The mind has a thousand eyes,
  And the heart but one;
Yet the light of a whole life dies
  When love is done.

Francis William Bourdillon

For permission to reproduce copyright material the publishers thank the following:
Warner Bros Music Ltd for the verse by Bob Dylan from 'To Be Alone With You',
copyright Big Sky Music; New Directions Publishing Corporation for the lines by
William Carlos Williams from 'The Unknown'; Faber and Faber Ltd and New
Directions Publishing Corporation for 'Song' from *Collected Early Poems of Ezra
Pound*, copyright 1976 by the Trustees of the Ezra Pound Literary Property Trust;
The International Bible Society for the excerpt from 1 Corinthians Chapter 13 from
The Holy Bible, New International Version; ATV Music Ltd and Northern Songs Ltd
for the lines from 'I Will' by John Lennon and Paul McCartney; Faber and Faber Ltd
and Harcourt Brace Jovanovich Inc for the lines from 'Pangloss's Song: A Comic-
Opera Lyric' from *Poems 1943-1956* by Richard Wilbur.